Discovering
JOBS

Jobs If You Like
ANIMALS

Don Nardo

ReferencePoint
Press®

San Diego, CA

For more information, contact:
ReferencePoint Press, Inc.
PO Box 27779
San Diego, CA 92190
www.ReferencePointPress.com

LIBRARY OF CONGRESS CATALOGING-IN-PUBLICATION DATA

Names: Nardo, Don, 1947- author.
Title: Jobs if you like animals / by Don Nardo.
Description: San Diego, CA : ReferencePoint Press, Inc., 2022. | Series:
  Discovering jobs | Includes bibliographical references and index.
Identifiers: LCCN 2021030392 (print) | LCCN 2021030393 (ebook) | ISBN
  9781678202248 (library binding) | ISBN 9781678202255 (ebook)
Subjects: LCSH: Animal specialists--Vocational guidance--Juvenile
  literature.
Classification: LCC SF80 .N37 2022 (print) | LCC SF80 (ebook) | DDC
  636.0023--dc23
LC record available at https://lccn.loc.gov/2021030392

CONTENTS

INTRODUCTION: LOST JOBS AND NEW OPPORTUNITIES

Following his usual routine, in the late afternoon one day in March 2020, Mark, a resident of Olympia, Washington, approached a well-kept house near the beach. As he did five times each week, he returned the two dogs he regularly walked to their owner. This particular day turned out to be different, however. "The owner thanked me," Mark recalls, "and said he was sorry, but with the ongoing coronavirus outbreak, he would be staying home from work for a while. He explained that he'd be doing a lot of his work from his house, so he'd be walking the dogs himself for the time being."[1]

Unexpectedly, therefore, Mark lost his job, or in this case *one* of his jobs. "Luckily for me," he adds, "that was my second job, not my main one. So I wasn't totally jobless. But I have a couple of friends who *did* lose their main jobs because of the virus."[2] Indeed, one of the largest side effects of the COVID-19 pandemic was that it threw tens of millions of people in the United States out of work. The difference between ordinary job losses in prior years and the losses during the pandemic was substantial. According to Lindsay M. Monte of the US Census Bureau, for example, in 2017 roughly 30 million Americans either lost their jobs or experienced a significant reduction in work hours. "In contrast," she points out, "roughly four times the number of people (115 million) had experienced a loss in employment income from the start of the pandemic in March 2020 through February 2021."[3]

Major Alterations in Procedures

Among those 115 million lost jobs were many that involved animals in one way or another. Suddenly out of work, or working fewer hours than usual, were dog walkers like Mark, seeing-eye

dog trainers, horseback riding instructors, zoo and aquarium attendants, and marine biologists, to name a few.

The pandemic affected other occupations related to pet care as well. As Mark discovered, pet groomers, walkers, and trainers suffered because many pet owners, who normally worked away from home in the daytime, now worked from home. As a result, the national pet care company Rover, which normally supplies the public with more than 1 million pet sitters each day, laid off over 40 percent of its workers in the pandemic's first two months. "If people are working from home and not traveling, the impact on our community of sitters and walkers is devastating,"[4] states the company's chief executive officer, Aaron Easterly.

Business was also down for nearly all organizations and facilities dealing with wild animals. High on that list were zoos and aquariums. For instance, the Oakland Zoo near San Francisco reported losses of some $2 million per month. On the opposite side of the country, meanwhile, the National Aquarium in Baltimore had to lay off a third of its staff. Similarly affected were the jobs of park rangers and wildlife managers in national parks. By mid-April 2020, the number of visitors to US national parks had declined by a whopping 87 percent.

Return to Normalcy?

Fortunately for all concerned, a fair proportion of such losses eventually reversed themselves as the pandemic largely wound down in the United States and parts of Europe in the spring and summer of 2021. Both zoos and national parks began to recover and to rehire workers who had been laid off. The Chester Zoo in Cheshire, England, was only one of dozens of zoos that brought back laid-off staff. Likewise, US national parks began to rebound. Officials at the Grand Canyon National Park in Arizona, for instance, reported an upsurge in visitors in April 2021, which in turn prompted rehiring many park personnel who had been laid off the previous year.

In the meantime, other people who made their living dealing with animals saw a steady return to some degree of normalcy in job opportunities. One outstanding example was that most workers in veterinary clinics who had been laid off during the first few months of the pandemic were quickly rehired. By the end of 2020, veterinarians across the United States reported that demand for pet care had greatly increased. In large part, they said, this was because millions of people who had been forced to stay home during the crisis adopted pets, all of which require standard veterinary care.

As jobs in veterinary clinics continued to multiply in 2021, still other animal-related occupations steadily rebounded. In Washington, for example, by the late spring of 2021 Mark started to get job offers from some of his former dog-walking customers. "Hopefully this trend will continue," he says. "At this point, considering what the whole country has been through, even if only half of my regulars come back, I'll count myself lucky."[5]

WILDLIFE BIOLOGIST

What Does a Wildlife Biologist Do?

A wildlife biologist is a scientist who examines, studies, and records the behaviors of animals, most often creatures that live in the wild. Wildlife biologists typically observe various natural ecosystems and how one or more animal species exists within those environments. They also determine, when possible, how those species interact with humans.

Frequently, wildlife biologists decide to specialize in specific areas of study based on certain animal species or groups of species. For instance, an ornithologist is a wildlife biologist who specializes in the lives of birds, an entomologist studies insects, paleontologists study prehistoric beasts by examining fossil records, and marine biologists examine the many species that dwell in the oceans.

Whether or not wildlife biologists have a specialty, they get involved in numerous aspects of the lives of the animals they work with and study. One common activity is to observe and manage a population of creatures inhabiting a given region. In such cases the biologist is expected to determine the approximate number of animals living within that region, what causes the local population to change over time (if it does), and the likely effects of that animal population on humans who live nearby. All such information is used in making decisions about how to manage the animals in question.

A Few Facts

Typical Earnings
Average annual salary of $60,000

Educational Requirements
Minimum of a bachelor's degree

Personal Qualities
Detail oriented, good problem solver

Work Settings
Office, classroom, outdoors in nature

Countering False Information About Animals

"As a biologist, I work frequently around misunderstood or feared animals. Unfortunately, bats which are highly beneficial to the ecosystem, fall under that umbrella. As biologists, the most prominent misconception we battle is the over exaggeration of the dangers of animals we work with. The media loves ratings and fear sells. Further, pseudo wildlife biologists feed into this fear mongering in an effort to make themselves look tough. As biologists, we actively respond to news stories that perpetuate false information of wildlife through fear-mongering. In most cases animals are nowhere near as dangerous as the general public has been led to believe."

—Jessie Story, wildlife biologist

Jessie Story, "Real Life Risk of Wildlife Through the Lens of a Wildlife Biologist," Outbound Collective, 2021. www.theoutbound.com.

In the course of this work, wildlife biologists sometimes humanely trap local animals for study or to tag and relocate them for their own good or the good of nearby human communities. Other typical activities and duties include devising ways to study and save endangered species, examining the spread of disease among the local animals, and coordinating with wildlife rehabilitators and fish and game agents who are helping manage those creatures.

Wildlife biologists approach all of these activities with the intention of ensuring that wild animals and humans in a given region can maintain their respective populations and hopefully live in harmony. Commenting on this key aspect of her job, wildlife biologist Mini Frkenswick Watsa explains that she and others in her profession "are doing the most important job of all—keeping this planet in homeostasis [a balanced state], so that others can continue to live in cities without facing drastic changes to their lives."[6]

Indian wildlife biologist Yashaswi Rao agrees. "My work," he says, "is crucial for ensuring a future where humans and wild ani-

mals co-exist. If we let things go unchecked, we would soon get to a point where our societal pressure on natural resources would drive these majestic creatures to extinction."[7]

A Typical Workday

Workdays for wildlife biologists can vary a great deal, depending on whether the person is working in a university classroom or office or out in the field. When working outdoors, the setting might be a forest, mountain, marshland, desert, or some other natural setting. For Watsa, such settings are often in Peru and other parts of South America. She describes her usual activities in the field, saying:

> When I'm in the field, my days are radically different than when I'm at home. While I'm in the forest, I wake each morning either before dawn or with the calls of duetting titi monkeys and I jump right into work. These days involve long hikes, chasing monkeys, and observation of behavior from a variety of vantage points. In the evenings, once the animals are asleep, I spend my day helping to transfer data into electronic files that are backed up in triplicate. By 9 pm, I'm in bed. Sleep is never more important than it is here.[8]

At home, in contrast, like other wildlife biologists, Watsa spends a good deal of time recording in writing the information she gathered firsthand in the field. "Occasionally I teach courses at Washington University in Saint Louis as well," she says, "and I confess that I spend a great deal of time in front of a computer." Considering that she enjoys fieldwork the most, Watsa says she is grateful that she is "never more than four months away from my next field adventure."[9]

Education and Training

To become a wildlife biologist, one needs at least a bachelor's, or four-year undergraduate, degree. More than that is preferable because an undergraduate degree will give someone seeking

a job as a biologist access to only an entry-level position. That initial degree can be in general biology, zoology, wildlife biology, ecology, or another related field, depending on what program a given university offers. Among the key courses one needs to pass are wildlife management, animal anatomy, statistics, and writing. Writing is essential for creating reports of one's biological fieldwork and composing papers for scientific journals.

To advance beyond entry-level positions, one needs a master's degree, and to obtain the most attractive job opportunities in the profession, getting a PhD is highly recommended. The wildlife biology candidate should also be adept at using computers, especially software programs that involve statistics and geographic information, which are basic to working with animal populations.

Skills and Personality

One of the most important skills wildlife biologists need to succeed is the ability to observe and remember details of the world around them. Typically, the job entails noticing small changes in an ecosystem or an animal's behavior and recording them later in writing. Good writing skills are a plus for this occupation because one needs to communicate with fellow scientists, as well as with students and sometimes the public. Good problem-solving skills are also beneficial because the natural world can be unpredictable. Sometimes, for instance, wildlife biologists need to quickly come up with ways to protect themselves or an animal from possible threats.

In addition, in regard to personality, it is vital that the would-be wildlife biologist have an innate interest in, or better yet love of, nature and the creatures inhabiting it. "I always had an affinity towards nature and wildlife," Rao says. "I always wanted to take the more unconventional path. . . . The biggest factor [in my decision to pursue this profession] was my own drive to pursue a [path] that could help me align my career with my passion for conservation."[10]

A wildlife biologist readies a captured great horned owl for relocation away from an airport in St. Louis, Missouri. Moving large birds away from airports protects the birds and the flying public.

Working Conditions

Working conditions can vary considerably for wildlife biologists. Sometimes they work in an office, classroom, library, or some other indoor setting, where reading, writing papers, teaching students, and other similar duties are required. In contrast, other times they work outdoors in the wild—in rain forests, on windswept prairies, and so forth—and often in a wide range of

An Occupation with No Typical Days

"The concept of 'typical day' does not exist in the field [of wildlife biology]. Every day is varied, owing to the dynamics of wild animals. But I usually spend a few hours in the forest at least 4 days a week. When I'm not in the forest, I work on data collection and analysis. I also liaise with forest department bureaucrats on a regular basis. The most enticing aspect of my work is the fact that I get to be in places where most people can't enter and do things most people would not be allowed to."

—Yashaswi Rao, wildlife biologist

Quoted in in Shyam Krishnamurthy, "Wildlife Biologist Interview," Interview Portal, 2020. https://theinterviewportal.com.

weather conditions. Reaching those natural settings may require extensive travel by plane or boat. It is important to stress, Watsa explains, that such travel is very different from the kind that people on vacation typically enjoy. "Actually," she says, for a wildlife biologist travel can be

> really, really hard. Ever tried to find a cat sitter for 3 months? Or attempted to clean a house that has been the playground for your cats for that long? In all seriousness, I feel like people envision a job that consists of airplane rides from one tropical beach town to the next, where I spend my spare time sipping on cocktails and enjoying the surf. In reality, I travel to one or two specific places every year to do a job, I eat less than stellar meals at a field site at which refrigeration is a luxury, and I work 16 hour days at a minimum. There are no cocktails involved at all, and certainly no beaches.[11]

Employers and Earnings

Some wildlife biologists work as professors at colleges and universities, while others are employed by towns, states, or the federal government to do research or various kinds of conservation work. There are also jobs open sometimes in the private sector—for instance, working for aquariums, zoos, or environmental research facilities.

The salary of a wildlife biologist can vary, depending on factors such as education level, the duties required, and whether the job is full time or part time. Low annual earnings for someone in this occupation range from $35,000 to $40,000; on the high end, meanwhile, a wildlife biologist with an advanced degree can make upward of $100,000 a year.

Future Outlook

According to the Bureau of Labor Statistics (BLS), the need for wildlife biologists will grow by around 8 percent by 2026, compared to a growth rate of about 7 percent for all occupations during the same period. Also, the BLS predicts, wildlife biologists who have advanced degrees will benefit from the highest number of career openings from 2022 to 2032. Moreover, the biggest demand for people in the profession will be in academia, or college settings. Another prediction by the experts is that a large proportion of the fieldwork of wildlife biologists in the 2020s and beyond will involve studies of how human population growth affects the animal kingdom in general.

Find Out More

National Park Service

www.nps.gov

The large National Park Service website offers much about the history of the national parks, how to plan trips to the parks, and how to help avoid forest fires and other dangers to parks. For young adults, there is information about the Youth Conservation

Corps, whose members work on park projects that promote appreciation of US public lands.

US Fish and Wildlife Service
www.fws.gov
This website contains valuable information on climate change, ongoing coastal projects, endangered species, new invasive species, conservation, and hunting and fishing. The website also provides information on job opportunities and how to do volunteer work.

Wildlife Society
https://wildlife.org
The Wildlife Society's mission is to allow wildlife biologists and other scientists to sustain wildlife habitats using sound management and conservation. The attractive website features the latest news about wild animals in the United States. Young people will find information about internships and jobs in wildlife management.

ANIMAL NUTRITIONIST

What Does an Animal Nutritionist Do?

Also sometimes called an animal nutrition scientist or a veterinary nutritionist, an animal nutritionist is a scientist who studies the physical and nutritional needs of animals and attempts to create balanced diets for them. A central aspect of the job is examining the caloric intake, level of activity, and overall condition and health of either a specific animal or an animal species. Often, the animal nutritionist finds that the nutritional requirements of one species will be very different from those of other creatures, despite the fact that they may seem related in some ways. For example, the food intake and dietary needs of dogs are quite different from those of cats, even though both are common pets that live in people's homes. Similarly, animal nutritionists have determined that the dietary needs of horses differ significantly from those of cows, sheep, and other common livestock.

The job entails detailed knowledge of animal anatomy and physiology, animal behavior, and the physical and economic factors involved in breeding, raising, and keeping animals. Animal nutritionists seek such knowledge about both domesticated creatures that live on farms or in homes and wild animals that dwell in zoos, aquariums, or nature reserves. In both acquiring and applying that knowledge, the nutritionist may variously develop feeding plans for certain animals; test new pet or livestock foods; determine the

---

A Few Facts

Typical Earnings
Average annual salary of $64,000

Educational Requirements
Minimum of a bachelor's degree

Personal Qualities
Good verbal and listening skills

Work Settings
Varied, including lab, office, classroom, and farm

---

chemical components and nutritional aspects of specific types of grass or other plants that might be useful in such foods; and give advice to owners of pets, livestock, or zoo animals about the most efficient diets available for those creatures.

Animal nutritionists are quick to point out that their occupation differs from that of experts who deal strictly with human nutrition. The reason, they say, is partly because most animals require different combinations of nutrients than people do. But it is also because humans can and often do eat whatever they want, even when it is not healthy for them. Animals generally do not approach food that way. In the words of Stewart Galloway, an animal nutritionist for Hubbard Feeds, "Animals have a perfect opportunity for good health and nutrition because they don't have the bad eating habits that some humans do."[12]

A Typical Workday

Although most animal nutritionists work full time, it is not always a so-called nine-to-five job. That is because some animal nutritionists, especially those who work on farms or for zoos or aquariums, have to be on call during evenings and weekends in case emergencies arise. In some cases animal nutritionists are expected to travel to other states and occasionally other countries. This happens, for instance, if nutritionists are asked (as they sometimes are) to teach about animal nutrition to zoo personnel, farmers, animal handlers in national parks, vets, or others who live in distant locations.

When not traveling, one of an animal nutritionist's most important duties is formulating diets and individual foods for a specific animal species. Nutritionists determine which ingredients will be best and in which proportions, as well as the proper amount of food an animal should be fed in a single sitting. They also help prepare the food labels—listing calories, fat, protein, and other items—that will appear on the package.

Another common task of animal nutritionists is to write articles about their products or animal nutrition in general. These end up

The Queen of Poop

"I think it's funny [that people call me the 'queen of poop']. Whenever I'm talking to anyone about almost anything, it always seems to come back to poop and what's going on in the gut. . . . The digestive tract is the center of everything. . . . There's so much in a pet's body that relates to what happens in their intestines, and nutrition plays such a large role in a pet's health. It's something that has fascinated me since I was in college. So, the title fits—I even refer to myself that way."

—Gail Czarnecki-Maulden, animal nutritionist

Quoted in Meagan Meehan, "Nutrition and Healthy Pets: Interview with Gail Czarnecki-Maulden, Ph.D.," Blasting News, November 14, 2017. https://us.blastingnews.com.

in diverse media outlets, including trade publications within the pet and livestock industries, print magazines, and online journals and blogs.

Some animal nutritionists spend their days doing research into innovative approaches to animal food and health. One of the leading animal nutritionists in the United States, Gail Czarnecki-Maulden, works for the Purina pet food company. In her job, her days often include exploration and testing of unproven ideas and products that might eventually be seen as beneficial. She says:

> We're empowered to pursue areas of work that are cutting edge, and our management encourages this. For a researcher, you can't ask for more than that. My role here is to work with a team of scientists who research the role of nutrition and its impact on pets' digestive health to help pets live long, healthy, and happy lives. We focus our efforts on examining key components of pets' poop to understand overall pet health and nutritional performance of food and treats.[13]

Education and Training

Animal nutritionists are almost always expected to have at least a bachelor's degree in a field related to nutritional work. Some of the more common college programs that candidates for the job tend to pursue are biology, veterinary studies, animal science, horticulture, and general nutrition. Enrolling in a college or university that offers an actual major in animal nutrition, such as Purdue University in Indiana or Canada's University of Manitoba, is a plus. Purdue's animal nutrition program is part of its distinguished Department of Animal Sciences, which features seven hundred undergraduate students, sixty graduate students, and thirty professors.

Quite a few animal nutritionists go on to get advanced degrees. Although a person can find a job in this field with only a bachelor's degree, graduate degrees are required for those who want to get involved in advanced research or management positions in companies that make food for animals.

It is also recommended that before or while attending college, individuals desiring to become animal nutritionists try to find some part-time entry-level positions in the profession. This may give them an edge later when applying for full-time work after earning a degree. Those entry-level jobs include working at aquariums, zoos, pet stores, and veterinary offices, all of which provide the person with hands-on experience with living animals.

Skills and Personality

Strong verbal and listening skills are useful qualities for animal nutritionists. In the course of their jobs, nutritionists may have conversations about diet and nutrition with farmers, veterinarians, zookeepers, and others involved in the care and feeding of animals. Consequently, it is important that they listen carefully and communicate clearly. Poor communication can lead to misunderstandings, which in turn can threaten animal health and well-being. Critical-thinking skills are also helpful because nutritionists often have only a minimal amount of data with which to effectively assess an animal's activity levels, habits, and dietary needs. The

nutritionist must be able to take that small amount of information and recognize patterns and connections in it and from that draw conclusions that will benefit an animal or group of animals.

According to the well-known online jobs website Career-Explorer, "Animal nutritionists have distinct personalities. They tend to be enterprising individuals [who are] ambitious, assertive . . . enthusiastic, confident, and optimistic. They are dominant, persuasive, and motivational."[14] Most people who know Czarnecki-Maulden see those sorts of qualities in her, and she says she picked up some of her spirited attitude from her college instructors. "When I went to Cornell as an undergrad," she recalls, "the enthusiasm of my professors and the innovative atmosphere spurred my interest in pet nutrition."[15]

Working Conditions

Work settings can vary considerably, depending on what kind of work animal nutritionists are doing at a given time. They may work in a lab, an office, or a classroom, for example. Or they may work on a farm or ranch that raises large numbers of domestic livestock, such as horses, cows, pigs, or sheep. In contrast, some animal nutritionists work from their homes as freelance consultants who are hired on a case-by-case basis.

Employers and Earnings

Most animal nutritionists work variously for pet food manufacturers, farmers, ranchers, aquariums, zoos, pet store chains, and some government agencies (such as the US Department of Agriculture). In addition, a small minority of people in this field are self-employed as consultants on a project-by-project basis.

Salaries for animal nutritionists also vary a lot. Entry-level nutritionists with a bachelor's degree can expect to make $40,000 to $50,000 a year. In contrast, an experienced nutritionist with an advanced degree can make $120,000 or more annually. According to the Bureau of Labor Statistics (BLS), the median yearly salary for members of the profession is about $64,000.

A Lightbulb Moment Leads to a Career

"During my undergraduate degree, I took a few human nutrition courses and found out I really liked nutrition. In my later undergraduate years where I had the opportunity to take more electives, I decided to take a few animal nutrition courses; fish nutrition, wildlife nutrition, and pet nutrition. I've always loved animals but didn't want to go the vet route, and when I took those courses it was a lightbulb moment for me."

—Natalie Asaro, companion animal nutritionist with pet food brand Petcurean

Quoted in Ontario Agricultural College, "Q+A with a Companion Animal Nutritionist," August 4, 2020. www.uoguelph.ca.

Future Outlook

The BLS estimates that employment for animal scientists is projected to grow from 8 to 10 percent by 2029, faster than the average for all occupations. Some experts estimate that as many as three hundred new animal nutritionist jobs will be created each year in the United States alone. Experts attribute much of that expected increase to a growing need to improve the diet and health of both pets and domestic livestock. Indeed, Czarnecki-Maulden predicts the advent of a number of "nutritional innovations over the next few years, and I plan to play a role in bringing those innovations to pet owners."[16]

Find Out More

American Academy of Veterinary Nutrition (AAVN)
www.aavnutrition.org
The AAVN is an international organization of animal nutritionists, veterinarians, scientists, pet industry representatives, and others who share an interest in the health of animals, both domestic and

wild. The website tells how students and other young people can get involved and start their own chapters of the AAVN.

American Society of Animal Science (ASAS)
www.asas.org
The ASAS works to foster the humane, effective use of animals to improve the state of human society. Students and other young people may be drawn to the website's colorful gallery of animal images and a section on fun facts about animals, including how to determine the temperature by counting cricket chirps.

Comparative Nutrition Society (CNS)
www.cnsweb.org
The CNS promotes better communication and sharing of knowledge among scientists of various kinds who are concerned with nutrition for both humans and animals. The group's website provides information about how students can take part in a poster-making competition that helps advertise the CNS's goals.

ANIMAL CONTROL OFFICER

What Does an Animal Control Officer Do?

Animal control officers investigate calls about sick or injured wildlife, as well as reports of animals attacking humans or other animals. Cases of animal cruelty also fall under the authority of animal control officers, and sometimes they must see that an animal gets proper medical care. In extreme cases—for example, if an animal is rabid—an officer may have to euthanize it, meaning put it down in a humane way.

Most animal control officers are quick to point out that a fairly large part of the job consists of combating ignorance on the part of animal owners. Indeed, Justin Foster, an animal control officer for Sonoma County in Northern California, says that a majority of cases of animal abuse he sees are caused by ignorance, rather than purposeful cruelty. He uses the example of horse owners, saying, "People don't understand how complex they [horses] are. They are expensive and require a lot of specialized care. People think they can just live off the land, and they can't."[17]

Scott Lowry, a supervising animal control officer for Nebraska's Lincoln-Lancaster County, agrees and says, "With neglect calls, when we do find a violation, we often can deal with it through education. There are a lot of people who own animals who don't know the basics of animal care. Our job is to tell them what city ordinances say, but also teach the correct way to care for an animal."[18] Overall, Foster

A Few Facts

Typical Earnings
Average annual salary of $46,000

Educational Requirements
High school diploma

Personal Qualities
Good physical condition, enjoy working with animals

Work Settings
All sorts, both inside and outside

says, he and other animal control officers enforce the local laws and regulations regarding animal ownership. "We don't *make* the laws," he explains. Although that part of the job can, at times, be very challenging, Foster adds, "I like the freedom of the job, the flexibility, working outside. I love the animals and being able to help them and to educate people about them."[19]

A Typical Workday

Animal control officers typically face many challenges and situations in a given day or week, so the job tends to be extremely varied. As Lowry describes it, "The variety of things I do from day to day is interesting. The fact that you never do the same thing really makes it fun for me. I've never been a person who likes to sit in the office. For me to get out and roam across the city responding to calls is ideal."[20]

The calls Lowry and other animal control officers respond to often deal with minor problems involving domestic animals. These can include cats locked in houses or caught in drainpipes, dogs or horses that seem malnourished or otherwise neglected, dogs biting people, and so forth. "A lot of people have a preconceived notion that we will seize a dog and destroy it if it bites someone," Foster says. "So they can be the most difficult people. They are actively obstructing you, trying to hide the dog."[21] When a dog does bite someone, he explains, first he tries to determine what led the dog to bite. He also determines whether the bite is part of a pattern, which might cause that animal to be labeled dangerous or vicious. The vicious ones are thereafter kept from being around people other than owners, doctors, and trainers. Occasionally, an officer like Foster gives his findings to a local judge, who ultimately decides whether the animal should be euthanized.

Another common duty is inspecting homes or businesses that have multiple animals and ensuring that animal owners have the proper licenses to keep a given number of animals. (The number varies from town to town, county to county, and state to state.) Sometimes animal control officers receive calls about hoarding.

This is when a person illegally keeps dozens, or even hundreds, of animals in their house. Often, hoarding cases involve cats or dogs, but animal control officers have also encountered hoarding of rats and other rodents, birds, and snakes and other reptiles. Conditions in houses where this happens are often abysmal—both for humans and animals. Animal control officers are animal lovers, so seeing these conditions can be emotionally challenging. According to Lowry:

> You're never ready for hoarding cases. Our main priority is to make sure we get all the animals out of these houses, and that requires us to keep ourselves safe by wearing protective gear. There's usually high ammonia levels associated with those that [hoard] cats. During the summer, because it's very hot and we're wearing all this protective gear, it can take a physical toll. The hoarders that we've come across in the past couple of years tend to have a lot of animals.[22]

Education and Training

Candidates for the job of animal control officer need to be at least eighteen years old and have a high school diploma or general equivalency diploma. Some towns, counties, and states prefer, though usually do not require, an associate's or bachelor's degree. Also, some states require that a candidate be specifically certified as an animal control officer, which entails receiving training in identifying, handling, and transporting animals. A number of states and towns offer such training, as do a few colleges. In addition, the National Animal Care and Control Association offers a training course that may be taken by anyone over age eighteen.

A person applying for a position in animal control also benefits from prior experience in a related field. This can include work as a police officer, assistant wildlife rehabilitator, veterinary technician, or animal shelter manager. Even simply volunteering at a local shelter can provide good real-world experience and look good on a résumé.

The Job's Potential Dangers

"Typically, there are three dangers: animal attack, assault by human, and the added danger of being around fast-moving traffic. The animals are the easiest to deal with. I'll take dogs for example. Dogs pretty much, under a given set of circumstances, will react the same way. . . . People are more unpredictable and harder to deal with. [Owners] often love their animals [as much as] their children. Sometimes our job requires that we take an animal and this causes stress."

—Scott Lowry, animal control officer in Nebraska

Quoted in Allison Hunter-Frederick, "Interview with an Animal Control Officer, Part 1," *Pet Talk: The Blog*, Lincoln Animal Ambassadors, April 12, 2017. https://lincolnanimalambassadors.wordpress.com.

Skills and Personality

Animal control officers should possess both physical agility and stamina. They tend to work on their feet for fairly long periods of time. Also, various aspects of the job require them to bend, stretch, and climb over or under a variety of obstacles to get to animals that need assistance.

In addition, from a psychological standpoint, an animal control officer should have two innate abilities. One is the capacity to deal with animals in a compassionate way; the other is the ability to deal with people, especially animal owners, in an evenhanded way. "It's hard to find someone who is good at both those things," Lowry points out. "I discovered that I was good at both of those things, and so I stayed [in the profession]."[23]

Another skill that comes in handy in the job is competency with various firearms. In most counties and states, animal control officers must become certified in their use, often including a shotgun and a .22 rifle. The reason is that one of their many duties is euthanizing a seriously injured creature, typically (though not always) with a .22 rifle.

A Maryland animal control officer poses for a photo with a dog she rescued from a neglect situation. Cases of animal cruelty and neglect fall under the authority of animal control officers.

It also benefits an animal control officer to have good writing skills. When dealing with criminal cases, for instance, officers are required to create a lengthy report that will be submitted to the local district attorney's office.

Finally, it is helpful for an animal control officer to sincerely care about the well-being of animals and be dedicated to curbing cruelty to animals. "The intentional cruelty cases are hard to shake," Foster says, "especially when it's been done to hurt someone else, because they know hurting the animal will hurt the person. But the silver lining is when you see accountability in action, when you've had a successful prosecution and you know justice has been served."[24]

Still, even when justice seems to have been served, the worst cruelty cases are impossible to forget, constituting one of the few drawbacks of the job. "You see things that are horrible," Lowry states, "and sometimes the things you see you can't believe you're seeing them. As much as you'd like to forget them, they're always in your head and mind. They stay with you."[25]

Working Conditions

Animal control officers face a wide range of working conditions, depending on where they live and work and the kinds of cases they deal with. If they live in a region that has dramatic winters, they will likely deal with snow and cold weather in the winter and be required to drive a lot on unpaved country roads. Forested areas, seacoasts, and of course densely populated urban areas all have their own unique climatic and physical conditions to which an officer will need to become accustomed.

No matter what the climate and topography of a region may be, the work will take an officer to a variety of human-made settings, ranging from homes, apartment buildings, and businesses to farms, factories, racetracks, and zoos. As with any occupation involving animals, working hours can be irregular. Most animal control officers are expected to remain on call so they can take care of emergency situations that may arise at night, on a weekend, or even on a holiday.

Employers and Earnings

Animal control officers are generally employed by a town, a county, or the federal government. In the cases of towns and counties, they often work alongside police officers.

The salaries of animal control officers vary quite a bit, depending on the economic conditions and local budgets of the states, regions, and towns in question. According to the Bureau of Labor Statistics (BLS), the average yearly salary for someone in the profession is in the neighborhood of $46,000. The top 10 percent of animal control offers earn as high as $82,000 annually, and the bottom 10 percent make about $26,000 per year or slightly less.

Future Outlook

The BLS estimates that demand for workers in the animal care employment sector will grow by as much as 22 percent during the mid- to late 2020s. That is considerably higher than the

An Animal Control Officer Speaks Out

"I always had a desire to be with animals. I grew up with animals all my life, and they've always been a passion of mine. . . . I enjoy working in this area [Los Angeles County, California]. It makes me happy. I love the community. [Also] every day I learn and experience new challenges. [For example] a lot of times, people are not happy to see us. [It can be difficult] having to explain to someone who is upset why I'm there at their home and to explain to them that our goal is always the well-being of animals."

—Julie Villegas, Los Angeles animal control officer

Quoted in Emily Alvarena, "It's Time to Thank the Animal Control Officers," The Signal, April 18, 2020. https://signalscv.com.

country's overall employment growth rate of 7 percent for all occupations in the country. The BLS does not predict the specific growth rate for animal control officers, but the fact that they are in animal care suggests that demand for them will grow during that period.

Find Out More

Animal Control Officers Association of Massachusetts (ACOAM)

www.acoam.org

Like similar groups in other US states, the ACOAM works to use education, training, and knowledge of applicable laws to promote the safety and security of animals and animal control officers alike. The website contains a list of the animals in the state and how to obtain fact-filled pamphlets about each of them.

California Animal Welfare Association

www.calanimals.org

This group promotes the passage of laws that mandate the humane treatment and general welfare of the state's animals, domestic and wild. The website features a section listing open animal welfare–related jobs, as well as one that explains how today's young people can become the leaders of future animal welfare efforts.

National Animal Care and Control Association (NACA)

www.nacanet.org

The NACA describes itself as an organization committed to setting the standard of professionalism in animal welfare. On the website, young people will find out how to enter the yearly photo contest (with pictures showing animal control officers aiding animals). Winning photos are displayed in a national magazine.

WILDLIFE REHABILITATOR

What Does a Wildlife Rehabilitator Do?

Wildlife rehabilitators help care for injured, orphaned, and abandoned animals with the goal of returning them to their natural habitats. People who do this job must have considerable knowledge about how to deal with various species of wild animals. Typical species that rehabilitators help include racoons, squirrels, groundhogs, deer, snakes, bats, and numerous kinds of birds.

If an animal is injured, a wildlife rehabilitator (or rehabber) figures out how bad the injury is and determines how likely it is that rehabilitation will be successful. If it does appear that the creature can be safely returned to the wild, the rehabber will administer necessary medical care, as well as physical therapy if that seems warranted. In more serious cases, in which the rehabber lacks sufficient medical knowledge, he or she generally consults a veterinarian.

Wildlife rehabbers all agree that helping orphaned, sick, and injured wild animals can be extremely rewarding. Christy Reeves, a rehabber in Canton, Georgia, recalls, "Eleanor the Groundhog was found by some people under a porta-potty. She was just 6 inches long and about 5 days old. I raised and took care of her for 3 months. She was my first groundhog and taught me a lot about how highly intelligent and wonderful these creatures are."[26]

A Few Facts

Typical Earnings
Average annual salary of $26,000 to $28,000

Educational Requirements
High school diploma; some college courses helpful

Personal Qualities
Feel compassion for animals, ability to tolerate difficult situations

Work Settings
Outdoors and inside rehab facilities or shelters

At the same time, the job can be very challenging and at times even emotionally upsetting. In the words of Amanda Margraves, the chief rehabber at the Florida Keys Wild Bird Rehabilitation Center, "The most challenging [part of the work] is definitely how much stress and death comes with the job. A lot of the animals that we see are very badly injured or very sick and do not survive. Dealing with death so often is a very stressful thing."[27]

Reeves points out another major challenge of the job; namely, educating the public. Well-meaning people sometimes attempt to rescue animals that appear to need help—but really do not. In these instances, the animals are behaving in ways that are normal for their species. Sometimes, she says, people see a young deer, or fawn, alone in the wild and think that the animal has been abandoned by its mother. "Their mothers usually appear for morning and evening feeding," she explains, "but people kidnap them." She also gives the example of baby birds that have fallen out of nests. "People think they need help but their parents have an eye on them and are trying to teach them to fly. But people kidnap them."[28]

A Typical Workday

Among the daily duties of a wildlife rehabber, the most common revolve around the day-to-day care of one or more animals in need. The rehabber feeds the creature, cleans up after it, and makes sure that it is in a safe situation in which it can properly recuperate. He or she also keeps an ongoing written record of each animal, listing its changing physical condition and any and all efforts that may go into aiding the creature.

Other typical duties of a rehabber may include teaching and overseeing volunteers, making phone calls to help raise funds to keep the rehab center functioning, and sometimes supervising a tour of the facility for interested members of the public. Engaging in these and other activities tends to keep the staff perpetually busy. Indeed, Margraves reports, "there is never a dull moment.

Each injury, each animal, each situation is different. It is definitely a fast paced job." She describes her typical day this way:

> I usually arrive at the center before anyone else around 5:30 am to check on very sick patients and to start feeding baby birds. My job consists of a lot of cleaning throughout the day. I also intake birds that people bring to us through-out the day. We coordinate rescue efforts for birds that the community calls about, we feed baby birds every 45 minutes throughout the day, we administer medications, weigh birds, do exams and checkups on birds as needed, deal with administrative stuff, write out protocols for new birds, train interns and volunteers and oversee their work, do surgeries or assist in major surgeries with our volunteer veterinarian, take phone calls from the public with ques-tions about local birds etc. We are also on call 24 hours a day . . . after we are finished at the center.[29]

Education and Training

There is no specific, widely offered college program in wildlife re-habilitation. So it is recommended that someone who is seriously considering this occupation try to get an undergraduate degree in a related field of study that will provide a good deal of information about animals and their needs. Possible appropriate programs include wildlife biology, zoology, ecology, animal behavior, orni-thology, and veterinary medicine.

That does not mean, however, that a college degree is always required to get a job as a wildlife rehabber. Many rehab facilities will hire someone who has a high school diploma and is willing to learn the trade over time through hands-on experience. In fact, whether one plans to go to college or not, volunteering at a rehab center is a good way to get started. In Margraves's words, "Vol-unteer! Start by volunteering at a local wildlife center. Although re-habbing may seem like something they want to do, a lot of people become burnt out very quickly and decide maybe it isn't the best

A Warning to Untrained People

"Rehabbing animals is a very difficult thing to do. There are many factors people don't realize that go into rehabbing an animal, including the proper medical care it needs, the proper diet, the proper housing while it recovers, and how important it is to not imprint an animal. I always recommend they call a licensed wildlife rehabber when they find a sick or injured bird. The sooner the bird gets to us the better chances it has for surviving."

—Amanda Margraves, wildlife rehabber in the Florida Keys

Quoted in Korrie Edwards, "Interview with Amanda Margraves: Head Wildlife Rehabilitator," Green Mind Initiative, June 5, 2015. https://thegreenmindinitiative.wordpress.com.

career choice for them. Volunteering helps them get experience and they can figure out if they really want to rehab."[30]

Skills and Personality

Anyone who works as a wildlife rehabilitator needs to have both an interest in and love for animals. These are usually people who tend to be sensitive, kind, curious, intellectual, and inquisitive. Many are also introspective, creative, and have feelings of empathy for other living things.

In these respects, wildlife rehabbing can be thought of more as a personal calling than a mere job. Margraves is only one of many rehabbers who see it that way. "I always wanted to work with animals," she says, and

> even when I was young, I went back and forth between [wanting to be] a veterinarian or a zookeeper. When I was in college I rescued an injured squirrel and it took me half a day calling people to finally get in touch with a wildlife rehabilitator. I didn't even realize this was something people did. After volunteering at a wildlife center I decided I wanted to be a rehabber.[31]

A Job That Can Be Stressful

"It's a 100% stressful and lonely job! . . . When you're under pressure to find money for animals that will be released back into the wild—so there's no return financially—it has a great impact on your mood and energy levels. The night feeds can be soul-destroying too, and when you're covered in bird poop, you stop taking care of your appearance and that has an effect on your self-esteem. There's definitely pros and cons to wildlife rehabilitation work."

—Kelly Wolmer, wildlife rehabber in England

Quoted in Rae Gallel, "Meet the Rescuers: An Interview with Kelly Wolmer, Founder of Runham Wildlife Rescue," *The Animalist* (blog), 2019. www.theanimalistblog.com.

Nevertheless, professionals in the occupation are quick to point out that having strong compassion for animals, though admirable and helpful, is not enough to succeed in the job. Much of what rehabbers do is not glamorous and consists of hard, often unpleasant work, including cleaning cages, dressing serious wounds, and when necessary, euthanizing suffering creatures. Thus, an ability to weather difficult situations and stark reality and still keep going from week to week is essential to the job. Skills such as safely capturing and handling wild animals in distress, administering first aid to them, and properly feeding creatures of diverse species are also essential but can be learned on the job.

Working Conditions

Although wildlife rehabbers sometimes work in the wild—usually when retrieving or releasing animals—most of the work happens indoors, in wildlife shelters or facilities. Kelly Wolmer, a rehabber in a suburb of London, England, states:

I spend all my life cleaning and feeding animals, along with vet trips and treatment. We have several aviaries [bird habitats], and will soon be expanding to a very large area, so just keeping everything clean and fed is a never-ending task. I can't go anywhere without monitoring the animals, so we have cameras in every room, and when I do go out I am usually accompanied by many hungry mouths! As a result, I tend to go out as little as possible.[32]

Employers and Earnings

Wildlife rehabbers work variously for government agencies, humane societies, nonprofit groups, and zoos. In some other cases, rehabbers obtain licenses to practice rehabilitation in their local towns and proceed to work with animals in their homes. Some rehabilitators specialize in specific types of animals, such as small mammals, birds, or reptiles.

Wherever they may do their work, wildlife rehabbers generally do not charge money for their services. (It is actually illegal to do so in some places.) As a result, rehabbers must rely on fund-raising and charitable donations to meet their operating expenses. Those expenses tend to include paying for cages and other habitats, medical supplies, food for the animals, blankets and towels, necessary visits to a local vet, and much more.

Because the money raised through donations must pay for so much, wildlife rehabbers themselves do not make large salaries. The average yearly earnings in the job in 2020 ranged from $26,000 to $28,000.

Future Outlook

Wildlife rehabilitation is a rapidly growing field, and new animal rehab facilities appear in the United States, Canada, Europe, and elsewhere regularly. The Bureau of Labor Statistics (BLS) does not single out wildlife rehabbers specifically but rather

lumps them together with other animal care and service workers. The BLS says that such workers will grow in number by a hefty 22 percent by 2029.

Find Out More
How to Find a Wildlife Rehabilitator, Humane Society of the United States
www.humanesociety.org/resources/how-find-wildlife-rehabilitator
This very useful website, sponsored by the Humane Society, lists wildlife rehab centers all around the United States and provides links to reach their individual websites.

International Fund for Animal Welfare (IFAW)
www.ifaw.org
The IFAW, with branches around the globe, rescues animals in crisis and works to preserve existing animal species. The website has a section that takes visitors around the world to see what the IFAW is doing, as well as a link to information on how individuals can help by contacting their senators and other leaders.

National Wildlife Rehabilitators Association (NWRA)
www.nwrawildlife.org
The NWRA works to improve and promote the profession of wildlife rehabbing and thereby to help humanity preserve the planet's natural ecosystems. The attractive website features a list of educational suggestions, advice on how to become a rehabber, and a list of ongoing job opportunities.

Wildlife Society
https://wildlife.org
The Wildlife Society's mission is to allow wildlife biologists and other scientists to sustain wildlife habitats using sound management and conservation. The attractive website features the latest news about wild animals in the United States. Young people will find information about internships and jobs in wildlife management.

VETERINARIAN

What Does a Veterinarian Do?

Veterinarians, often called simply "vets" for short, are medical practitioners who specialize in maintaining and improving the health of animals, including domestic pets, livestock, and in some cases wild animals. The pets range from dogs and cats to hamsters, guinea pigs, rabbits, mice, rats, birds, snakes, and lizards, among others. Vets also routinely advise owners on how to properly care for pets and livestock. Some of the typical specific duties performed by vets are diagnosing various symptoms of illness though direct examination, X-rays, and other means; dressing wounds; doing surgical procedures; giving vaccinations for rabies and other diseases; prescribing medication; and when necessary, euthanizing animals.

As many vets will attest, the job can be both fascinating and challenging. One area that can be particularly difficult but also rewarding is diagnostics. "That is a real fulfillment for myself," says Houston, Texas, vet Aubrey Ross, "because what we're doing is we're helping the animals that can't speak for themselves." Indeed, an animal is unable to "tell you where it hurts," Ross says. It cannot express in words, as humans can,

A Few Facts

Typical Earnings
Average annual salary of $99,000

Educational Requirements
Bachelor's degree plus four years of veterinary school

Personal Qualities
Good communications skills, a willingness to work hard

Work Settings
Mostly indoors in a veterinary clinic

whether they're feeling better or whether you're doing the right thing. You have to rely on the owner, you have to rely on the sixth sense. Diagnosing sick animals is the most challenging part of it all. Diagnosing and being able to have a working relationship with that animal to know whether it is doing better, and taking history from the fifteen to twenty minutes you spend with a person [owner] in there.[33]

A vet who gave an anonymous interview to Job Shadow, a website that investigates and describes diverse careers, points out that another central benefit of the job is the gratifying feeling that can come from saving an animal. (The vet in question chose anonymity because he wanted to frankly describe the downsides of the profession without having a debate with fellow vets.) "When you save an animal's life," he states, "or some little old lady comes in here and gives you a hug because you have saved her animal's life, that's what it's all about."[34]

A Typical Workday

Most veterinarians work full time at a minimum, and it is common in the profession to work more than forty hours per week. It is also typical for vets to put in extra time on some weeknights, as well as weekends. This is because it is often necessary for them to respond to emergency calls to aid animals in crisis. Ross describes a typical day for himself and his two colleagues, saying:

It starts at 7 and doesn't end until roughly 8 or 9 at night. . . . We open at 8. We close at 5. Emergency animal control brings in different types of emergencies, hit by cars, neglect cases, and we can't leave until the last patient is seen. So we're here all the time. We're working all the time, and then we try to spend that quality time [that is left] with our families, with our kids, with our wives, to try and find that common balance.[35]

A veterinarian performs a routine exam on a canine patient. Some vets specialize in livestock while others care mostly for pets. Dogs and cats are the most common pets seen by these vets but they also care for pet rabbits, birds, rats, and lizards, among other animals.

Education and Training

Anyone interested in becoming a veterinarian needs to prepare for a lot of schooling. In addition to a high school diploma, a would-be vet must get a bachelor's degree in an area of animal studies, such as zoology, wildlife biology, or ornithology. Then he or she must attend veterinary school for four years to acquire a DVM (doctor of veterinary medicine) degree.

In addition to those eight years of rigorous schooling, vets have to be licensed in order to practice in the United States. Licensing requirements vary from one state to another. However, all would-be vets in the country are required to pass the North American Veterinary Licensing Examination (NAVLE), administered by the International Council for Veterinary Assessment, headquartered in Bismarck, North Dakota. The NAVLE is known for being extremely comprehensive and difficult to pass. Most would-be vets do pass it on their first or second try, but a few take it three or more times before passing it. The maximum number of tries allowed is five.

Skills and Personality

The vet interviewed by Job Shadow provides this general overview of the sorts of personal qualities that make for a successful veterinarian:

> A person should like sciences, they should like math, they should like to work hard, have as high a grade point average as you can have, and most of them have to [get some practical experience by working] for a veterinarian, either during summer or during their four years before they get into school. You have to have some degree of intelligence. You have to apply yourself and be able to make a four point grade average or as high as you can get to a four point average.[36]

As for specific abilities, it helps for a vet to have strong communication skills. This is because explaining treatment options and conveying other important information to animal owners is an essential aspect of the job.

Also, a vet should feel genuine compassion for animals in need and sympathy for owners whose pets or livestock are sick or deceased. Indeed, the animals in a vet's care and their own-

The Worst Part of the Job

"Every animal is different. Sometimes it's surgery that they need and the [owner] can't afford the surgery and the decision has to be made. But most of the time it's animals that are very sick with cancer, or their life has just come to a stage where their quality of life isn't good any more, so you humanely put them down . . . and they fall asleep peacefully. But that *is* hard."

—Jamie Kelly, veterinarian on Canada's Prince Edward Island

Quoted in NEXT Network, *Interview—Veterinarian Dr. Jamie Kelly*, YouTube, October 26, 2012. www.youtube.com/watch?v=ZKWN8XJmeuM.

ers should always be treated with kindness and respect. Good decision-making skills are also helpful because vets regularly have to make life-and-death decisions about their patients. In addition, considerable manual dexterity is a plus because vets routinely treat injuries and perform surgery, both of which require detailed and precise use of the hands.

Finally, a would-be vet should be willing to work hard on a consistent basis. This is partly to gain experience but also to build up a practice. In the words of the Job Shadow interviewee, one needs to have what might be called a burning desire to be a veterinarian. "It ain't an 8-5 job," he quips, and

> there are many times you have to put in longer hours. I'd say that most veterinary students come away from school with about $150,000 in debt, and that takes a lot out of your income to start with. It's a difficult road the first five years out of school. You just don't come out of veterinary school and say, "Here I am. I'm a veterinarian," you know, and you're going to get this big salary, and life is going to be great. It's not. The person needs to have patience, and want, and have a desire. There has to be that desire to be a veterinarian.[37]

Why Become a Vet?

"It's a great profession. But let's be realistic, let's go in with our eyes open. . . . I found out over 40 years, that I get very cautious about hiring or working with a person who says 'Why did I want to be a veterinarian? Because I like animals more than people.' That's a red flag for me because [in] veterinary medicine . . . we have to be people persons *and* animal persons. I got into this profession because I love people *and* animals. . . . This is a profession where you serve both populations."

—Mark Goldstein, veterinarian

Quoted in Zazie Todd, "Interview with Dr. Mark Goldstein," *Companion Animal Psychology* (blog), July 17, 2019. www.companionanimalpsychology.com.

Working Conditions

Most veterinarians work indoors in private clinics and hospitals. Some travel to farms, ranches, or zoos, and others work in classroom settings as professors in colleges that have veterinary programs. Some vets specialize in large animals, such as horses, cows, or even elephants. Such specialists tend to spend much of their time not only on farms or at zoos but also at racecourses or other places where large animals are found.

A typical veterinary clinic has a front waiting area and a front desk or business office where pet owners check in. The bulk of such a clinic consists of exam rooms, areas with cages to hold visiting animal patients, and sometimes an on-site lab to do blood tests and other lab work.

The conditions in a veterinary clinic can sometimes be on the messy and smelly side. The holding cages for the animals get soiled and need to be cleaned regularly, and employees are routinely exposed to blood, urine, and so forth. Although entry-level clinic employees take care of cleaning the cages and exam

rooms in most cases, the vets occasionally need to tend to such duties themselves.

Employers and Earnings

Most vets work for themselves or in a practice with other vets, but a few are hired by government agencies and zoos. According to the Bureau of Labor Statistics (BLS), in 2020 the median yearly earnings of veterinarians was about $99,000. The highest-earning 10 percent of vets that year made around $164,000, and the lowest-earning 10 percent made about $50,000.

Future Outlook

According to the BLS, employment for veterinarians will likely expand by up to 16 percent by 2029, much faster than the average for all occupations. CareerExplorer offers the following reasons for that expected growth, beginning with

> rising incomes and the increase in the number of people aged 34 to 59, historically the highest pet owner demographic. The rise in pet insurance purchases indicates that pet owners also may be willing to pay for more elective and intensive care than in the past. In addition, demand for veterinarians is growing as a result of the ongoing development of scientific methods of breeding and raising livestock, poultry, and fish.[38]

Find Out More

American Animal Hospital Association (AAHA)

www.aaha.org

The AAHA seeks to provide the highest quality of care for companion animals by improving standards of care. It also accredits, or endorses, veterinary hospitals. The website offers detailed information about getting an education in veterinary medicine, including how to become a veterinarian.

American Veterinary Medical Association (AVMA)

www.avma.org

The AVMA works to advance the science and practice of veterinary medicine in order to improve animal and human health. The comprehensive website contains information about which colleges offer veterinary programs, how students can apply for internships with veterinary practices, and ongoing job openings.

United States Animal Health Association (USAHA)

www.usaha.org

The USAHA's main goal is to ensure the health of livestock and prevent diseases that negatively affect the livestock of ranchers, farmers, and consumers. The website features detailed information about various animal diseases and chronicles the latest news about breakthroughs in scientific efforts to eliminate those diseases.

VETERINARY TECHNICIAN

What Does a Veterinary Technician Do?

A veterinary technician, often called a "vet tech" for short, is in a sense a veterinarian's nurse or assistant. Vet techs have many typical duties, among which are performing initial examinations of animals arriving at a clinic, setting up surgical equipment for an upcoming operation to be performed by the vet, collecting various specimens from incoming animal patients to be examined in the on-site lab, actually doing those lab procedures, drawing blood from animals, gathering medical histories from the owners, providing emergency first aid when necessary, and assisting the vet in doing research into rare conditions and diseases that can affect animals. Lindsay Calhoun, a vet tech in Wyckoff, New Jersey, describes her many duties:

> As an assistant in the exam room, I meet with pet owners to talk about the reason for their visit and record their pet's weight and medical history. I assist the vet during the appointment with tasks such as retrieving medications and controlling the animal during the exam, if needed. Working in the pharmacy, I fill prescriptions, prepare controlled substances, and restock medications. When I am scheduled to help with surgeries, I do things like prepping the animal, starting the IV, and monitoring the anesthesia.[39]

A Few Facts

Typical Earnings
Average annual salary of $35,000

Educational Requirements
Associate's or bachelor's degree

Personal Qualities
Good communication and organization skills

Work Settings
Mostly in veterinary clinics

Saving an Animal's Life

"[In a particularly satisfying experience on the job] we once took in a cat that had been in a house fire. He had been burnt pretty badly and . . . had also lost half an ear. The owner had taken him to another clinic first, where the veterinarian concluded that he needed to be euthanized. [Fortunately] the owner called our clinic for a second opinion. Our vet elected to try to save him. . . . His ear didn't grow back, but he did regain all his hair and recover fully otherwise. . . . The owner still has the cat, named Probie."

—Mary Mould, veterinary technician

Quoted in All Allied Health Schools, "Interview with a Veterinary Technician." www.allallied healthschools.com.

Mary Mould, a vet tech and program coordinator at Vet Tech Institute's Pittsburgh campus, provides some input of her own: "This is a field where you can really make a difference! A veterinary technician job involves taking care of animals in hospitals and clinics by prepping them for surgery, drawing blood and placing catheters. During a surgical procedure, techs are always on hand to administer anesthesia, monitor patient heart rates and temperatures, and assist the vet."[40]

In addition to these higher-profile duties, vet techs do sometimes have to perform more mundane tasks, including some decidedly unglamorous ones. Being a vet tech can sometimes mean "getting your hands dirty and doing some grunt work," Calhoun explains. "No matter which part of the [clinic] I'm scheduled to work in, I always have to do things like clean out cages, wipe down tables, sterilize instruments, and clean up messes."[41]

A Typical Workday

In a busy veterinary practice, the vet tech's day can be very full. Olivia, a vet tech at Dedham Veterinary Associates in Dedham,

Massachusetts, usually starts her workday by 7:00 a.m. and ends her workday around 8:00 p.m. She says:

> Usually my first duties involve admission of patients to the hospital for surgery. Working with a doctor, we perform exams and collect vitals and come up with a plan for anesthetic drugs. Technicians need to know a lot about drugs and anesthesia to come up with the safest anesthesia for each pet. The morning is then full of placing catheters, administering and monitoring anesthesia, recovering patients from surgery, and managing them post-operatively. We always try to leave a little time in the day to make sure everyone gets a chance to eat something, but often it is only a moment for a quick bite to eat before a transition to helping with appointments. Appointments involve a lot of talking to pet owners about heath and preventive care topics, collecting and sorting through medical information, obtaining blood, urine and fecal samples and performing less-than-fun procedures, like expressing anal glands. . . . My day normally ends no earlier than 8 pm, when I get to go home, exhausted, a bit bruised and scratched, but feeling fulfilled, and ready to snuggle with my own pets.[42]

Education and Training

In most cases someone who desires to become a vet tech should earn either an associate's degree—which involves two years of study—or a bachelor's degree—which takes four years. Programs for veterinary technicians exist in about 230 colleges and universities in the United States, and a number of similar programs can be found in colleges in Canada, the United Kingdom, and several European nations.

Most veterinary technician training programs require that a student complete a hands-on internship in order to obtain his or her degree. In such cases the student works for a while in a

veterinary clinic and receives a grade and/or written evaluation by the vet in charge of the clinic. Besides being a requirement, such an internship provides the would-be vet tech with invaluable real-world experience as well as something to add to a résumé when applying for jobs later.

Most states also require entry-level vet techs to be state certified, and that involves passing a rigorous exam. The most common exam of this type is the three-hour-long Veterinary Technician National Exam. It consists of 170 multiple-choice questions.

Skills and Personality

A vet tech should have effective communication skills, in part because she or he regularly confers with and gets crucial information from pet and livestock owners. Good organizational skills are also preferred, as is being detail oriented. This is because in a typical day, there are many animals needing care in a veterinary clinic; each has specific characteristics and needs, so there is a good deal of information to sift through and keep track of.

Also, being a compassionate person who cares about animals and their welfare is a given for this occupation. As Calhoun puts it, "I have always loved animals and been interested in helping them. When I was a kid, I rode horses and had dogs, cats, lizards, fish, and a guinea pig. I also took in and cared for a few stray animals. Being around a variety of animals throughout my life has definitely helped prepare me for working at an animal hospital."[43]

An effective vet tech should also be willing to do hard work on a regular basis. In Mould's words, "A vet tech's job is not all about playing with little kittens and puppies. This is a great field, but a hard job. It really isn't about playing. In the end, it is about veterinary medicine, and to pursue this you must really want to make a difference."[44]

A Calling Rather than a Job

"This is a calling for me. There has never been anything else I have ever wanted to do. When I was applying to colleges I only applied to the two colleges in Massachusetts that had vet-tech programs, knowing that I would accept nothing else. . . . I did not apply for a plan B because there is nothing else I would want to do. Being a veterinary technician is everything to me."

—Olivia, vet tech at Dedham Veterinary Associates in Dedham, Massachusetts

Quoted in Dedham Veterinary Associates, "Interview with a Veterinary Technician," November 12, 2020. https://dedhamvetassociates.com.

Working Conditions

A majority of vet techs work in standard private veterinary clinics owned or run by one or more licensed veterinarians. These tend to be fairly large structures with many individual rooms, including exam rooms, labs, rooms containing cages to house the animal patients, offices, and so forth. Most of the patients tend to be small animals, like dogs, cats, guinea pigs, and mice. But a few such clinics are geared toward larger animals, such as pigs and horses. Whatever animals a vet tech may deal with, he or she can expect to spend most of a typical day within the confines of the clinic, moving frequently from room to room. The degree of cleanliness ranges from fairly spotless waiting rooms and exam rooms to a much messier caging area that must be cleaned regularly.

Employers and Earnings

In addition to being employed in veterinary clinics owned and/or run by veterinarians, vet techs can sometimes be found working in university or government labs that do biomedical research involving animals, the veterinary departments of zoos, companies involved in the health management of livestock, and the facilities run by various humane societies. In addition, a few vet techs work

for large pharmaceutical companies or end up teaching courses in community colleges and other schools of higher learning. Mould, for instance, began her career in a veterinary clinic and later found a teaching position at a local college.

Salaries earned by vet techs usually depend on one's level of experience. Beginners in the field may earn around $24,000 to $27,000 per year, whereas someone with several years of experience can earn $50,000 or more annually.

Future Outlook

According to the Bureau of Labor Statistics (BLS), veterinary medicine is a highly in-demand professional area. Various projections by the BLS and other groups that study labor trends estimate that the number of viable jobs for vet techs will increase in number by 16 to 20 percent by 2029. That is a considerably faster growth rate than the average for all jobs. It means that the approximately 115,000 working veterinary technician jobs in the United States in 2021 could increase to well over 140,000 during the 2020s.

Several factors contribute to this highly positive career forecast. First, in recent years veterinary medicine has become increasingly advanced and now features more treatment options for pets and livestock than in the past. Some of the specialized treatments now routinely offered in large numbers of clinics in which vet techs work include imaging and chemotherapy. Also, animal care in general is expanding each year. Over 90 million US families owned pets in 2020, most of which required some sort of veterinary care.

Find Out More

American Veterinary Medical Association (AVMA)
www.avma.org
The AVMA works to advance the science and practice of veterinary medicine in order to improve animal and human health.

The comprehensive website contains information about which colleges offer veterinary programs, how students can apply for internships with veterinary practices, and current job openings.

Association of Zoo Veterinary Technicians (AZVT)

https://azvt.org

The AZVT is dedicated to promoting high-quality veterinary technical care in the field of zoo animal medicine by sharing ideas and contributing to conservation in the wild. The website tells how students can obtain scholarships and internships and get involved in programs that offer hands-on experience.

National Association of Veterinary Technicians (NAVTA)

www.navta.net

NAVTA strives to provide both would-be vet techs and existing vet techs with detailed, up-to-date information about the profession. The website contains a section on how one can become educated as a vet tech and a section on obtaining scholarships and other student resources.

SOURCE NOTES

Introduction: Lost Jobs and New Opportunities

1. Mark, personal interview with the author, May 22, 2021.
2. Mark, interview.
3. Lindsay M. Monte, "Historical Look at Unemployment, Sectors Shows Magnitude of COVID-19 Impact on Economy," U.S. Census Bureau, March 15, 2021. www.census.gov.
4. Quoted in Revell Horsey, "Pet Care in a Post-pandemic World," *Forbes*, December 28, 2020. www.forbes.com.
5. Mark, interview.

Wildlife Biologist

6. Quoted in Ben Lybarger, "Meet a Field Biologist: Interview with Dr. Mini Erkenswick Watsa," Field Projects International, 2021. https://fieldprojects.org.
7. Quoted in Shyam Krishnamurthy, "Wildlife Biologist Interview," Interview Portal, 2020. https://theinterviewportal.com.
8. Quoted in Lybarger, "Meet a Field Biologist."
9. Quoted in Lybarger, "Meet a Field Biologist."
10. Quoted in Krishnamurthy, "Wildlife Biologist Interview."
11. Quoted in Lybarger, "Meet a Field Biologist."

Animal Nutritionist

12. Quoted in Iowa Agriculture Literacy Foundation, "A Day in the Life of an Animal Nutritionist," April 7, 2021. https://iowaagliteracy.wordpress.com.
13. Quoted in Meagan Meehan, "Nutrition and Healthy Pets: Interview with Gail Czarnecki-Maulden, Ph.D.," Blasting News, November 14, 2017. https://us.blastingnews.com.
14. CareerExplorer, "What Does an Animal Nutritionist Do?," 2021. www.careerexplorer.com.
15. Quoted in Meehan, "Nutrition and Healthy Pets."
16. Quoted in Meehan, "Nutrition and Healthy Pets."

Animal Control Officer

17. Quoted in Heather Bailey, "A Day in the Life of an Animal Control Officer," SoCoNews, January 23, 2017. https://soconews.org.
18. Quoted in Allison Hunter-Frederick, "Interview with an Animal Control Officer, Part 1," *Pet Talk: The Blog*, Lincoln Animal Ambassadors, April 12, 2017. https://lincolnanimalambassadors.wordpress.com.
19. Quoted in Bailey, "A Day in the Life of an Animal Control Officer."
20. Quoted in Hunter-Frederick, "Interview with an Animal Control Officer, Part 1."
21. Quoted in Bailey, "A Day in the Life of an Animal Control Officer."
22. Quoted in Hunter-Frederick, "Interview with an Animal Control Officer, Part 1."
23. Quoted in Hunter-Frederick, "Interview with an Animal Control Officer, Part 1."
24. Quoted in Bailey, "A Day in the Life of an Animal Control Officer."
25. Quoted in Hunter-Frederick, "Interview with an Animal Control Officer, Part 1."

Wildlife Rehabilitator

26. Quoted in Robs Rescues, "Interview with Christy Reeves: Small Wild Thing Savior." https://robsrescues.com.
27. Quoted in Korrie Edwards, "Interview with Amanda Margraves: Head Wildlife Rehabilitator," Green Mind Initiative, June 5, 2015. https://thegreenmindinitiative.wordpress.com.
28. Quoted in Robs Rescues, "Interview with Christy Reeves."
29. Quoted in Edwards, "Interview with Amanda Margraves."
30. Quoted in Edwards, "Interview with Amanda Margraves."
31. Quoted in Edwards, "Interview with Amanda Margraves."
32. Quoted in Rae Gallel, "Meet the Rescuers: An Interview with Kelly Wolmer, Founder of Runham Wildlife Rescue," *The Animalist* (blog), 2019. www.theanimalistblog.com.

Veterinarian

33. Quoted in Hollywood Soapbox, "Interview: *Animal Planet*'s 'Vet Life' Follows Three Vets as They Save Animals," June 4, 2016. www.hollywoodsoapbox.com.
34. Quoted in Job Shadow, "Interview with a Veterinarian," 2021. https://jobshadow.com.
35. Quoted in Hollywood Soapbox, "Interview."
36. Quoted in Job Shadow, "Interview with a Veterinarian."
37. Quoted in Job Shadow, "Interview with a Veterinarian."
38. CareerExplorer, "The Job Market for Veterinarians in the United States," 2021. www.careerexplorer.com.

Veterinary Technician

39. Quoted in Sara Royster, "Veterinary Technician: Lindsay Calhoun," *Occupational Outlook Quarterly*, Spring 2014. www.bls.gov.
40. Quoted in All Allied Health Schools, "Interview with a Veterinary Technician." www.allalliedhealthschools.com.
41. Quoted in Royster, "Veterinary Technician."
42. Quoted in Dedham Veterinary Associates, "Interview with a Veterinary Technician," November 12, 2020. https://dedhamvetassociates.com.
43. Quoted in Royster, "Veterinary Technician."
44. Quoted in All Allied Health Schools, "Interview with a Veterinary Technician."

INTERVIEW WITH A WILDLIFE REHABILITATOR

Kristin Fletcher is the executive director of the Wildlife Rehabilitators Association of Rhode Island. She has worked as a wildlife rehabilitator for over twenty years. She answered questions about her career by email.

Q: Why did you become a wildlife rehabilitator?

A: Even as a child I had a strong connection to animals and grew up around lots of pets. I became a wildlife rehabilitator following Hurricane Bob (in 1992), when my young daughters brought home an infant squirrel that they found in the road amongst some downed tree branches. At that time, I found it impossible to find help for the little guy and attempted to research proper care. Unfortunately there were very limited resources in our state. Ultimately, I was able to release him back into the wild, but at the time I had a gut feeling that there was so much I probably did improperly.

Q: Can you describe your typical workday?

A: There really is no "typical" workday for wildlife rehabilitators because we are on call from start to finish, for all manner of wildlife emergencies and issues involving animals. The variables can often seem endless! Year round, the day always begins with animal care for those wild patients who I am caring for at home. During our wild baby season (in Rhode Island each year the baby season runs from March into October), the care is constant from dawn to dark. For instance, the youngest baby songbirds require feedings every fifteen minutes, squirrels need to be fed every couple of hours, bunnies require food three times per day, etc. It is a constant merry-go-round of feeding, cleaning, not to mention

phone calls from the public about other babies in need. Most often, members of the public are able to deliver the animals to us, but on occasion we have to attempt to find transport on our own.

Q: What do you like most about your job?
A: The best part of my job is being in the position to be able to help each animal that I receive. Sometimes that means setting broken bones, rearing orphaned babies until they are healthy, and treating all sorts of illnesses. Sometimes it is the ability to be able to end incredible suffering by employing humane euthanasia (humanely putting an animal to sleep) in cases in which an animal cannot be fixed and is in great pain. It is so clear that they are suffering needlessly. And I like being part of the solution, especially knowing that the bulk of the animals we receive are injured or orphaned due to a number of negative human impacts, including being hit by cars, getting entangled in power lines, getting injured in construction sites and places where people are doing tree work, and of course abuse to pet cats and dogs by their owners.

Q: What do you like least about your job?
A: I would say that the very worst part of my job is dealing with animals' extreme traumas and the inability to save every example of wild life I receive for care. There is always the worry in the back of my mind that I could have done something differently or that I missed something along the way, when a wild patient dies. Regardless of how many wild lives are saved, those who die leave the longest impression on me.

Q: What personal qualities do you find most valuable for this type of work?
A: I find, having been a wildlife rehabilitator for 22 years, that the most valuable qualities one can have are commitment, respect for all forms of life, and a strong desire to keep learning. Wildlife rehabilitation is absolutely a 24 hour endeavor, and it can affect every part of your life. If you have wild babies of any sort in your

care, your days are strictly mapped out for you and that does not include things like trips to the beach, weddings, funerals, and an array of general outings. Indeed, just doing my grocery shopping can be a huge challenge! Fortunately, baby season lasts for a few months only, and the rest of the year is far more manageable in terms of a wildlife rehabilitator's time commitment.

Q: What advice do you have for students who might be interested in this career?

A: Since home rehabilitators are trained and licensed volunteers, students would need to consider finding a paid position with a wildlife facility. Many of our staff at The Wildlife Clinic have degrees in wildlife management, wildlife biology, or environmental sciences, but none of those are prerequisite to being hired as a wildlife rehabilitator. What is required for that is training in wildlife rehabilitation, whether it be in-person classes or virtual programs of one kind of another. Most states have very strict requirements for handling wildlife, which include specific training, apprenticeships with experience rehabilitators, and testing, which leads to licensing in that particular state only. Once licensed, many people continue to train to work with various animal species. Separate licenses, with associated targeted training, may be required to handle different species, like rabies vector species (for example, foxes, racoons, and bats), raptors (birds of prey, like hawks), and large predators (like wolves and bears).

OTHER JOBS IF YOU LIKE ANIMALS

animal cruelty investigator
animal rights activist
animal shelter manager
animal shelter technician
animal trainer
aquarist
beekeeper
conservation biologist
conservation officer
dog or cat breeder
dog walker
farrier
fish and game warden
horseback riding instructor
K9 unit trainer
marine biologist
marine mammal trainer

park ranger
pet adoption counselor
pet groomer
pet photographer
pet store associate
seeing-eye dog trainer
snake venom milker
veterinary acupuncturist
veterinary anesthetist
veterinary assistant
veterinary dentist
veterinary pathologist
veterinary sales
   representative
veterinary surgeon
wildlife conservationist
zoo veterinarian

Editor's note: The online *Occupational Outlook Handbook* of the US Department of Labor's Bureau of Labor Statistics is an excellent source of information on jobs in hundreds of career fields, including many of those listed here. The *Occupational Outlook Handbook* may be accessed online at www.bls.gov/ooh.

INDEX

PICTURE CREDITS

ABOUT THE AUTHOR

Classical historian, amateur astronomer, and award-winning author Don Nardo has written numerous volumes about scientific topics, including *Destined for Space* (winner of the Eugene M. Emme Award for best astronomical literature); *Tycho Brahe* (winner of the National Science Teaching Association's best book of the year); *Planet Under Siege*; *Climate Change*; *Deadliest Dinosaurs*; and *The History of Science*. Nardo, who also composes and arranges orchestral music, lives with his wife, Christine, in Massachusetts.